How were castles built? What was it like to live inside a castle? How did knights defend castles from enemy attacks?

Find out the answers to these questions and more in...

Magic Tree House Research Guide #2
KNIGHTS AND CASTLES

A nonfiction companion to
The Knight at Dawn

It's Jack and Annie's very own guide to the Middle Ages.

Including:
- Fairs and feasts
- Tournaments
- Battles and sieges
- Arms and armor

And much more!

Magic Tree House Books

#1: DINOSAURS BEFORE DARK

#2: THE KNIGHT AT DAWN

#3: MUMMIES IN THE MORNING

#4: PIRATES PAST NOON

#5: NIGHT OF THE NINJAS

#6: AFTERNOON ON THE AMAZON

#7: SUNSET OF THE SABERTOOTH

#8: MIDNIGHT ON THE MOON

#9: DOLPHINS AT DAYBREAK

#10: GHOST TOWN AT SUNDOWN

#11: LIONS AT LUNCHTIME

#12: POLAR BEARS PAST BEDTIME

#13: VACATION UNDER THE VOLCANO

#14: DAY OF THE DRAGON KING

#15: VIKING SHIPS AT SUNRISE

#16: HOUR OF THE OLYMPICS

#17: TONIGHT ON THE *TITANIC*

#18: BUFFALO BEFORE BREAKFAST

#19: TIGERS AT TWILIGHT

#20: DINGOES AT DINNERTIME

#21: CIVIL WAR ON SUNDAY

#22: REVOLUTIONARY WAR ON WEDNESDAY

Magic Tree House Research Guides

#1: DINOSAURS

#2: KNIGHTS AND CASTLES

Magic Tree House
Research Guide #2
KNIGHTS
AND CASTLES

A nonfiction companion to
The Knight at Dawn

by Will Osborne
and Mary Pope Osborne

illustrated by Sal Murdocca

A STEPPING STONE BOOK™
Random House 🏠 New York

www.randomhouse.com/magictreehouse

Library of Congress Cataloging-in-Publication Data
Osborne, Will.
Knights and castles / by Will Osborne and Mary Pope Osborne ; illustrated by
Sal Murdocca. p. cm. — (Magic tree house research guide #2) "A Stepping
Stone Book." SUMMARY: Jack and Annie look at knights, armor, and life in a
castle. ISBN 0-375-80297-5 (pbk.) — ISBN 0-375-90297-X (lib. bdg.)
1. Knights and knighthood—Europe—Juvenile literature.
2. Castles—Europe—Juvenile literature.
3. Civilization, Medieval—Juvenile literature.
[1. Knights and knighthood. 2. Castles. 3. Civilization, Medieval.]
I. Osborne, Mary Pope. II. Murdocca, Sal, ill. III. Title. IV. Series.
CR4529.E85 O84 2000 940.1—dc21 99-49811

Printed in the United States of America July 2000 10 9 8 7 6 5 4 3

Random House, Inc. New York, Toronto, London, Sydney, Auckland

For Anthony Herrera

Historical Consultant:

DR. MIKE NORRIS, Associate Museum Educator, The Metropolitan Museum of Art, New York, New York.

Education Consultant:

MELINDA MURPHY, Media Specialist, Reed Elementary School, Cypress Fairbanks Independent School District, Houston, Texas.

We would also like to thank Dr. Jack Hrkach at Ithaca College for providing information on medieval theater; Paul Coughlin for his imaginative photography; and at Random House: Cathy Goldsmith and Joanne Yates for their design work, Meredyth Inman for her research assistance, Mallory Loehr for her help and support, and again, our editor, Shana Corey, for her enormous contribution to this series.

KNIGHTS
AND CASTLES

Contents

1. The Middle Ages   13

2. The Age of Castles   21

3. Protecting the Castle   31

4. Castle Life   41

5. Festivals and Fairs   55

6. Knights   63

7. Armor   75

8. Weapons   85

9. Battles and Sieges   93

10. The End of the Age of Castles   103

Doing More Research   108

Index   116

Dear Readers,

Our adventures in the Magic Tree House always make us want to know more about the places we visit.

When we got back from the time of knights and castles in <u>The Knight at Dawn</u>, we wanted to know more about dungeons. We wanted to know more about armor. We wanted to know more about what goes on inside a castle.

To find out, we needed to do <u>research</u>.

We went to the library. We found pictures of famous castles in the encyclopedia. We checked out books

about the Middle Ages. The librarian helped us find facts about knights on the Internet. We even found a video about building a castle!

Now we want to share our research with you. So get your notebook, get your backpack, and get ready to gallop across the drawbridge into the time of knights and castles.

Jack

Annie

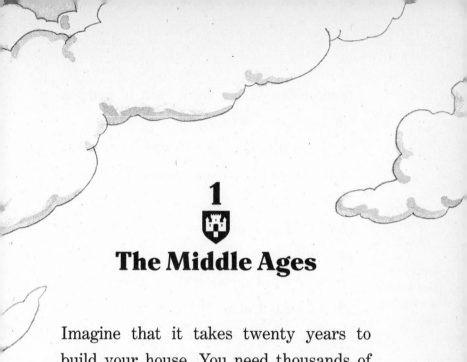

1

The Middle Ages

Imagine that it takes twenty years to build your house. You need thousands of workers to build it. You need hundreds of servants to run it. You need a small army of armored men to protect it.

Welcome to the time of knights and castles.

We often read about make-believe castles in fairy tales and legends.

The real castles that are most like the

ones in fairy tales were built in Europe during the *Middle Ages*.

The Middle Ages began about 450 A.D. They lasted for over 1,000 years. This period of history is called the Middle Ages because it was between ancient times and modern times. It is sometimes also called the *medieval era*. *Medieval* is Latin for "middle age."

Eyeglasses were invented in the Middle Ages!

The Middle Ages were a time of great change in Europe. More people learned to read and write. The first universities were built. New kinds of painting and poetry were created.

A university is a school of higher learning.

The Middle Ages were also a time of war and fighting. People fought with each other about religion. They fought about who should marry who. Mostly, they fought about land.

Battle of Agincourt, 1415.

During the Middle Ages, nearly all the land in Europe belonged to kings. Each king's land was called his *kingdom*.

Most kingdoms were too big for a king to defend without help. So a king often turned over pieces of his kingdom to men he trusted. These men were called *barons*. The pieces of land were called *fiefs* (FEEFS), or *manors*.

Some manors were very large. They could include several villages and many farms.

A baron didn't own his manor. But he ruled over all the people who lived and worked there. And he could build a castle on the manor for himself and his family.

In return, a baron *swore allegiance* to the king. That meant he was willing to die to protect the king and the kingdom.

The baron also promised to send soldiers to fight for the kingdom if it were attacked. These soldiers were called *knights*.

Not all knights got their own manors. Some lived in a lord's castle.

Knights swore allegiance to the king *and* the baron. In return, knights were often given their own manors to rule over.

Most of the people who actually worked on the land were called *serfs* (SURFS). Serfs didn't rule over anyone.

They had almost no rights at all.

Serfs were allowed to farm a tiny bit of land. They were allowed to keep some of what they grew to feed their families. They had to give the rest to the lord who ruled over them.

Anyone who ruled over land and the people on it was called a lord.

In return, most serfs also worked in their lord's fields. Some worked in his household. Some even helped build the lord's castle.

This system of trading the use of land for loyalty and work during the Middle Ages is called the *feudal* (FYOO-dul) *system*.

Feudal System

King

Barons

Knights

Serfs

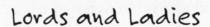

Lords and Ladies

In the Middle Ages, most rich people were *nobles*. Nobles came from families that had been wealthy for a long time.

Noble women were called *ladies*. They could also have titles, such as baroness, duchess, or countess.

Lady Annie,
Countess of Pennsylvania

Lord Jack,
Duke of Frog Creek

Noble men some-mes had titles such as baron, duke, or count.

The feudal system helped keep order during the Middle Ages. But it wasn't very fair.

A person almost always had to be born into the nobility. Even people who worked very hard and became rich could not normally become nobles.

Today in Europe, America, and many other places around the world, people are free to try to be almost anything they want.

Cardiff Castle, Wales.

2

The Age of Castles

Castles were an important part of the feudal system. They were built to protect lords and their land from enemy attackers.

Nobody knows exactly when the first castle was built. But the busiest time for castle building in Europe began about 1050 and lasted until the end of the Middle Ages.

The word castle comes from the Latin word castellum, which means "fortress."

So many castles were built during

this period that historians sometimes call it "The Age of Castles." By the end of the Age of Castles, there were over 12,000 castles in Europe.

The First Castles

The first castles looked more like forts in the Old West than castles in fairy tales. They were built out of wood.

These castles were usually built on a mound of earth called a *motte* (MAHT). They had a tower called a *keep*, a yard called a *bailey*, and a tall fence called a *palisade* (PAL-uh-sade).

Motte

Keep

Bailey

Palisade

Wooden castles could be built very quickly. Some were built in less than a week! But wooden castles didn't always protect a lord from his enemies.

Enemy armies could break through wooden fences. They could burn down wooden buildings.

Stone was a much better defense against attack. So by the 1100s, most castles were being built out of stone.

Building a Stone Castle

Building a stone castle was a lot more work than building a wooden one.

Tons of stone had to be dug out of the ground. There were no bulldozers. All the digging had to be done by hand.

The heavy stones had to be pulled on wagons or carried by boat to where the

This kind of castle is called a motte and bailey castle.

castle was being built. Loading and unloading the boats and wagons was a huge job.

The actual stonework on the castle was done by men called *masons*.

A *master mason* worked with the lord to plan the castle. He also made sure all the other castle builders did a good job.

Freemasons and *rough masons* carved the stones and cut them into blocks.

Each mason had a special mark that he often carved into the stones he cut. Carving the special mark was like signing a painting.

Carpenters did all the wood-work for the castle. As the stone walls got higher and higher, the carpenters built *scaffolding* (SKA-ful-ding) so the stoneworkers could reach the top.

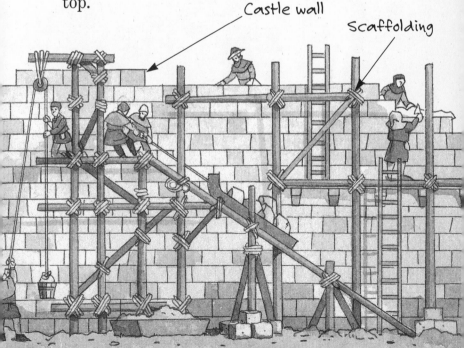

Castle wall

Scaffolding

Nails and tools were made by *black-smiths*. Blacksmiths also fixed broken tools. They stayed busy because tools broke a lot.

The master masons, carpenters, and blacksmiths who worked on a castle were all *master craftsmen*. They had spent many years learning to do their jobs well.

Master craftsmen often had *apprentices* (uh-PREN-tuh-siz). Apprentices were assistants who were learning to become master craftsmen.

The master craftsmen and their apprentices needed lots of help. Most of their helpers were poor people who lived near the castle site.

Castle Builders' Jobs

Masons

Carpenters

Blacksmiths

Apprentices

Building a stone castle sometimes took more than twenty years. By the time a castle was finally finished, over a thousand people might have worked on it.

How to Become a Master Craftsman

1. Become an *apprentice* to a master craftsman. Run errands and work without pay. Learn skills.

2. After about seven years, become a *journeyman* (JUR-nee-mun). Practice your skills. Work for low pay.

3. Make something that shows off your skills (it's called your *masterpiece*). Present your masterpiece to a *guild*. (A guild is a group of master craftsmen who share the same skills.)

4. Congratulations!

Your work has passed the guild's test!

You can now be a member of the guild and train apprentices of your own!

Jack
of
Frog Creek
Master Craftsman

3

Protecting the Castle

It took a lot longer to build a stone castle than a wooden one. It also cost much more.

Most lords thought stone castles were worth the extra time and money. When a stone castle was complete, it was *very* hard for an enemy to get inside.

Stone castles often had towers that reached high above the walls. There were watchmen in the towers. When the watchmen saw an enemy coming, they blew horns to sound an alarm.

Sentries (SEN-treez) with bows and arrows stood guard along the tops of all the castle walls. The sentries were protected by stone *battlements* (BAT-ul-munts). Battlements had gaps called *crenels* (KREN-ulz) and solid places called *merlons* (MUR-lunz).

When the sentries heard the watchmen's alarm, they could shoot arrows at the enemy through the crenels. If the enemy shot back, the sentries could duck behind the merlons.

Crenel

Merlon

Sentry

Battlements

If the enemy got past the tower watchmen, they still had a long way to go to get inside the castle.

Tower

Watchman

First they had to go through the *barbican* (BAR-bih-kon). The barbican was a walled passage that led to the castle gate. There were big doors on each end. If the enemy tried to sneak into the castle, guards could close the doors. The enemy would be trapped!

Yikes! Some moats may even have had crocodiles!

If the enemy got through the barbican, they then had to cross the *moat* (MOTE). The moat was a deep, wide ditch that ran all the way around the outside of the castle walls. The moat was usually filled with water.

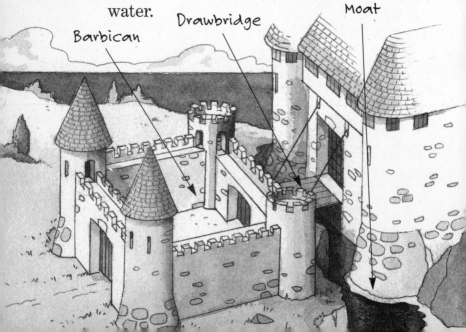

Barbican

Drawbridge

Moat

The only way to cross the moat was to go over the *drawbridge*. The drawbridge worked sort of like a seesaw. When it was lowered, it made a bridge from the barbican to the castle gate. When it was raised, it blocked the gate—and there was no other way across the moat.

A sliding door made of iron bars also protected the castle gate. The door was called a *portcullis* (port-KUL-iss).

Portcullis

Behind the portcullis was a pair of big wooden doors. The doors were very thick. They had strong bolts.

When guards at the castle gate heard the alarm, they raised the drawbridge. They lowered the portcullis. They shut the doors behind the portcullis. They locked the bolts on the doors.

It was almost impossible for the enemy to get inside the castle!

Turn the page to see how all the different parts of a castle fit together.

Watchtower

Crenel

Mews

Keep

Merlon

Moat

Stables

A castle wasn't just the building where the lord lived with his family. It was <u>everything</u> that was built to protect the lord and his land.

Sentry walk

Gatehouse

Portcullis

Barbican

Well

Drawbridge

4

Castle Life

A castle wasn't built just to protect people from their enemies. For the lord and lady of the manor, the castle was also home.

A lord and lady usually married at a very young age. Most boys and girls from noble families were married by the time they were fourteen years old.

Noble marriages were often arranged by the couple's parents. Sometimes the bride and groom didn't even meet each other until their wedding day!

Once they were married, the lord and lady each had many duties.

The lord was in charge of the whole manor. He was a general, police chief, and judge all rolled into one. He protected the people who lived on the manor. He also collected taxes from them. He settled arguments and punished criminals.

The lady of the manor ran the castle household. She made sure all the servants did their jobs well. She took care of castle business when the lord was away.

For fun, lords and ladies often went hunting together. Some also sang and played musical instruments. Many played the game of chess.

Many lords and ladies kept falcons for hunting. The building where the falcons lived was called the <u>mews</u>.

43

The lord and lady's children were usually sent to live in other castles when they were about seven years old. There they learned manners and school lessons. It was feared their parents would spoil them if they stayed at home.

Hundreds of servants lived in a castle. Their job was to keep the lord and lady as

comfortable, safe, and happy as possible.

Some servants worked in the kitchen. They roasted meat and baked bread. Other servants washed clothes and swept floors.

Special servants helped the lord and lady dress and bathe. It was considered a great honor to be chosen as a personal servant to the lord or lady.

Lords and ladies often dressed in very fancy clothes. Ladies almost always wore long dresses. Married women were supposed to keep their hair covered at all times. A lady's head-dress could be *huge!*

A <u>tunic</u> is a loose-fitting piece of clothing usually worn over a shirt or blouse.

Lords usually wore hose made of wool and shirts made of linen. They often wore *tunics* (TOO-nicks) over their shirts. They sometimes wore floppy hats with very long tails.

Shoes with pointed toes were also popular. Some shoes were so long and pointed that they were twice as long as the wearer's feet!

The lord and lady did not take baths very often. When they did, their servants filled a giant wooden tub with water heated over a fire. They used soap made from ashes and sheep's fat.

The lord and lady slept in a big bed in the master bedroom of the castle. The bed was usually very fancy, with curtains all around it. When the lord visited other castles, he often took his bed and his bathtub with him!

Beds were high to keep mice out.

The Great Hall

The Great Hall was the biggest room in the castle. It was where the lord settled arguments among the people who lived on the manor. It was where he met with important visitors. It was also where the lord's family, his knights, and his guests ate their meals.

At mealtimes, the hall was lit by candles and torches. There was often a huge fire blazing at one end of the hall.

At the other end of the hall was the *high table*. The high table was set on a platform. It was where the lord and lady ate their meals. Their food was served on plates made of pewter or silver or gold.

<u>Pewter</u> is a metal made of tin mixed with copper and lead.

Everyone else sat on benches or stools at long wooden tables. There were no plates for them. Their meals were served on thick slices of stale bread. The bread slices were called *trenchers* (TREN-churz). When the trenchers got too soggy to hold meat, they were given to beggars outside the castle.

Table manners were a little different than they are today. There were no forks, so it was all right for people to eat with their fingers. Several people might drink from the same cup. They could throw their scraps on the floor. It was even okay to spit on the floor!

By the end of a meal, the floor of the great hall was really dirty. It was covered with scraps of food, bones, and even droppings from animals. Servants sometimes spread flowers and dried weeds on the floor to cover the bad smells.

On holidays and other special occasions, the castle had celebrations called *feasts* (FEESTS). On feast days, the Great Hall was filled with music. Singers and musicians performed while the guests ate. Jugglers and jesters also entertained the crowd.

Cooks worked night and day preparing fancy dishes for a feast. They might roast peacocks and serve them with all their feathers. They might serve a swan with its beak painted gold.

Sometimes a cook would put live birds inside a pie. When the pie was cut open, the birds would fly out!

Turn the page to attend a medieval feast.

THIS WAY

5

Festivals and Fairs

Some of the most exciting events on the manor were religious festivals and trade fairs.

Religious festivals took place on holidays, such as Christmas and Easter. There were often feasts in the Great Hall. The lord gave most of the workers on the manor the day off. Townspeople sometimes performed in the villages. They acted out stories from the Bible.

The word holiday comes from the words holy + day.

Religion in Everyday Life

Religious worship was also an important part of everyday life during the
Middle Ages.

Most castles had their own chapels. The chapel was often the most beautiful room in the castle. Many chapels had stained-glass windows, painted walls, and crosses made of gold.

Castles usually had their own priest, too. Each morning, the lord and lady prayed in the chapel with the priest. The priest said a blessing before every meal. He conducted weddings and other religious services.

Kings and noblemen also gave money to build large churches called cathedrals. Some cathedrals were bigger than castles!

Most lords also built churches for the serfs who lived on their manors.

Sometimes the lord and lady of the manor went on a religious *pilgrimage* (PIL-grim-ij). A pilgrimage is a trip to a holy place. People believed that making a pilgrimage would help them get to heaven when they died.

Market Days and Trade Fairs

Of course, not all gatherings on the manor were religious. There were also market days and trade fairs.

A **merchant** is a person who buys and sells goods.

Market days usually happened once a week. On market days, farmers and merchants set up stalls outside the castle gate. People on the manor came to buy food, clothes, and other goods.

Trade fairs happened once or twice a year. At trade fairs, merchants from around the world came and set up tents. They sold everything, from candles and soaps to fancy daggers and swords. People from nearby villages sold pies and cakes and hot wine. Minstrels walked through the crowd, singing songs. Their songs often told stories of heroes and their adventures. There

A **minstrel** was a medieval singer and musician.

were even trained dogs and bears that
would dance for pennies.

Everyone on the manor looked forward
to market days and trade fairs. On these
days, they could take a break from their
daily chores. They could shop. And they
could gossip and share news with their
neighbors and friends.

Turn the page to
visit a medieval
trade fair.

THIS WAY

59

Merchant
stall

Cloth from the
Far East

Juggler

Minstrel

Dancing-bear

Acrobat

Swords from Spain

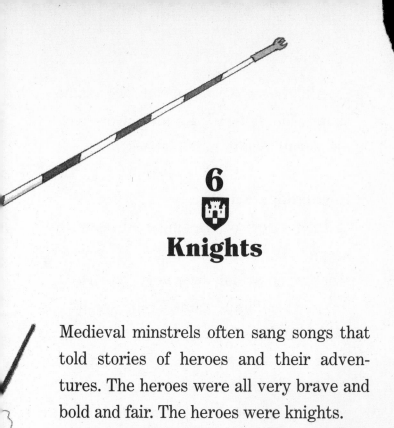

6

Knights

Medieval minstrels often sang songs that told stories of heroes and their adventures. The heroes were all very brave and bold and fair. The heroes were knights.

Knights had different names in different countries. In Spain, they were called *caballeros* (kab-uh-YER-os). In Germany, they were called *Ritters* (RIT-urz). In France, they were called *chevaliers* (shuh-VAL-yayz).

All these words mean the same thing: "horsemen." Knights were soldiers who fought on horseback.

Becoming a Knight

It took years of training to become a knight. It also took a lot of money. Horses and armor were very expensive. So most knights came from wealthy, noble families.

Not fair! Only boys could become knights.

A boy who wanted to be a knight started his training when he was about seven years old. At that time, his parents sent him to live in another lord's castle. He became a page.

A page served the lord's family their meals. He learned manners. He learned battle skills by fighting with wooden swords and riding on wooden horses.

Wow! Jack could be a page!

When a page was about fourteen, he became a *squire* (SKWIRE). A squire was an apprentice to a knight.

A squire took care of his knight's horses. He polished his knight's weapons and armor. If a knight were called to war, his squire went with him.

A squire had to be ready to fight beside his knight on the battlefield. So he practiced fighting with real swords and other weapons. Most important, he practiced his *horsemanship*.

Horsemanship means "horse-riding skill."

A squire had to learn to ride a horse without using his hands. On the battle-field, he would need both hands to hold his weapons and shield.

Most squires became knights at about age twenty-one. They were usually knighted at a *dubbing ceremony*.

A squire could be dubbed, or knight-ed, by his father or by the knight who trained him. A squire from a very important family might even be dubbed by the king himself!

At the dubbing ceremony, the new knight promised to be brave and loyal. He swore to protect his lord, his king, and his church.

Becoming a Knight
Page
Squire
 (Dubbing Ceremony)
Knight

Chivalry comes from the French word cheval, which means "horse."

The Code of Chivalry

In the later Middle Ages, knights also promised to have good manners.

They had to be fair to all people. They had to protect the weak. They had to be generous. They had to honor and respect women.

These rules came to be called the *Code of Chivalry* (SHIV-ul-ree).

In real life, knights could be ruthless and cruel. But the minstrels' songs of heroes reminded them of the Code of Chivalry and how they had promised to behave.

Turn the page to read about the most famous knights of all.

THIS WAY

King Arthur and the Knights of the Round Table

During the Middle Ages, the most popular stories about knights were tales of King Arthur and his kingdom of Camelot. They were make-believe stories. But they may have been based on a real king who lived in Britain in the sixth century.

One of the most famous stories about King Arthur is that of the *Sword in the Stone*. In the story, the people of Britain find a stone with a sword thrust into it. Writing on the stone says: WHOEVER CAN PULL THE SWORD FROM THIS STONE IS THE TRUE KING OF BRITAIN. A young page named Arthur is the only one who can pull the sword out of the stone.

Merlin

The person who put the sword in the stone was Merlin, a magician. After Arthur is crowned king, Merlin becomes his most trusted adviser. Merlin helps Arthur start the Knights of the Round Table. Arthur's knights gather at a table that is round so that each knight's place has the same worth.

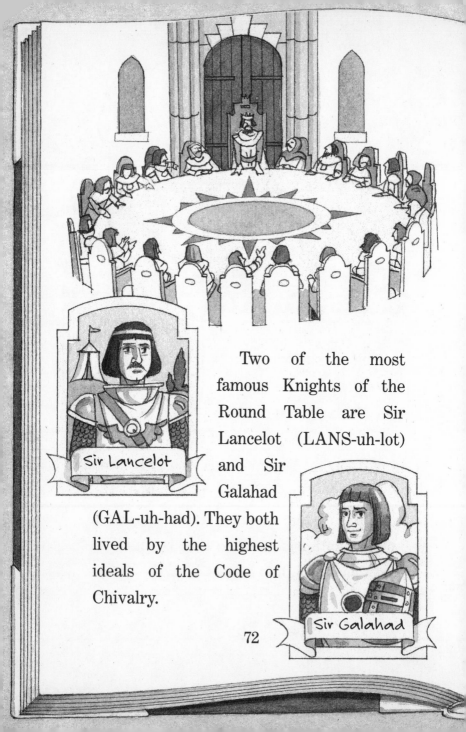

Two of the most famous Knights of the Round Table are Sir Lancelot (LANS-uh-lot) and Sir Galahad (GAL-uh-had). They both lived by the highest ideals of the Code of Chivalry.

Sir Lancelot

Sir Galahad

72

Two important women in the stories of King Arthur are Queen Guinevere (GWIN-uh-veer) and Morgan le Fay (MOR-gun luh FAY).

Guinevere is the beautiful wife of King Arthur.

Queen Guinevere

Morgan le Fay

Morgan le Fay is the half sister of King Arthur. She learns magic skills from Merlin, such as how to fly and how to change her shape.

Full plate armor.

7

Armor

As part of his dubbing ceremony, a new knight was often given a suit of armor. Armor is metal covering that protected a knight from his enemy's weapons.

Armor was heavy. It was hot. It was hard to put on and take off. But it was the best protection a knight could have when he went into battle.

The earliest armor was made of small metal rings all linked together. The linked rings were called *mail*. Mail was first popular in the eleventh century.

This kind of armor is often called <u>chain mail</u> because the rings are linked like a chain. ⟶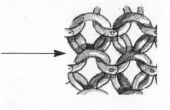

Knights going into battle wore a mail coat called a *hauberk* (HO-burk).

A hauberk was good protection against the sharp edges of a sword. But a knight could be stabbed through the mail rings with a thin *dagger*.

Hauberks were so heavy that knights who wore them had to wear padded underwear!

He could also be shot with an arrow, or have his bones smashed with a heavy club.

To better protect themselves, some knights started strapping steel plates over their mail armor.

A **dagger** is a short pointed weapon.

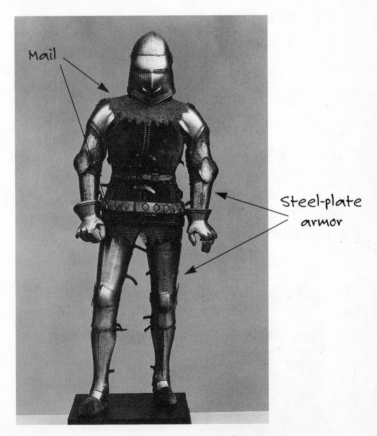

Mail

Steel-plate armor

Steel plates were much better protection than mail rings. By the 1400s, most knights no longer wore mail at all. Instead, they wore steel-plate armor that covered them from head to toe.

Helmets

One of the most important pieces of a knight's armor was his helmet. Like all armor, helmets changed over time. The earliest helmets were simply steel hats with nose guards.

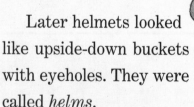

Later helmets looked like upside-down buckets with eyeholes. They were called *helms*.

In the fourteenth century, knights began wearing helmets called *basinets* (bass-uh-NETS). Basinets fit more closely around the knight's head. Most had *visors* that moved up and down. That way, the knight could see better when he wasn't fighting.

Tournament helmets were sometimes very fancy—and heavy! Some tournament helmets weighed over forty pounds.

A Suit of Armor

There were so many pieces in a full suit of
steel armor that it could take over an hour
for a knight to get dressed. Knights in full
armor even wore steel gloves and steel
shoes!

Chest plates

Horses wore armor, too. A horse's armor was called a *bard*.

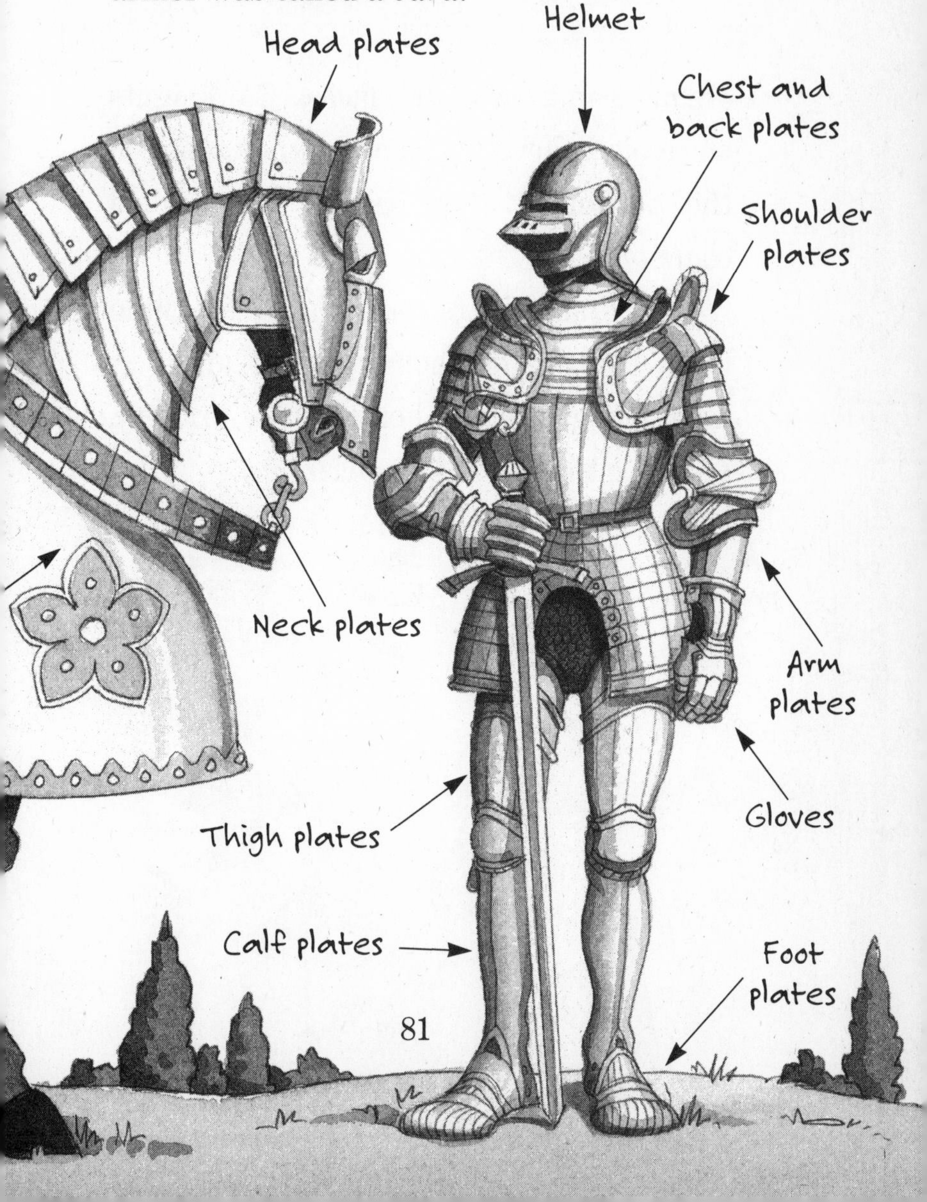

Head plates

Helmet

Chest and back plates

Shoulder plates

Neck plates

Arm plates

Gloves

Thigh plates

Calf plates

Foot plates

81

Jack and Annie Present:
The Story of Heraldry!

Helmets hid knights' faces. So knights wore big badges to tell each other apart on the battlefield. The badges were called *coats of arms*.

The first knights could choose anything they wanted for their coats of arms. A knight might pick a lion to show bravery, or a tree to show his strength.

Annie
the oak

Jack
the owl

82

Eventually, though, there weren't enough pictures to go around.

Annie
the sun

Jack
the sun

Strict rules were made about who could use which pictures. There were also rules about how the pictures could be drawn.

Annie the
bluebird

Jack the
jaguar

The person who checked to make sure the rules were being followed was called a *herald*. The whole system of coats of arms is called *heraldry* (HERR-ul-dree).

Battle of Poitiers.

8

Weapons

A knight carried many weapons into battle. His most important weapon was his sword.

Early swords were flat and wide. They had two sharp edges. They were called *slashing swords*.

Armor did a good job of protecting knights from the sharp edges of slashing swords. So sword makers started making swords that were longer and more pointed than slashing swords. These swords were

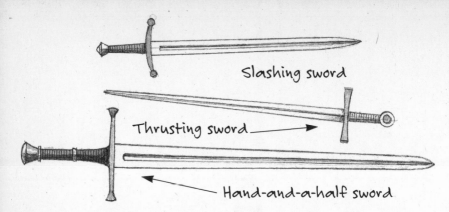

Slashing sword

Thrusting sword

Hand-and-a-half sword

called *thrusting swords*. The point of a thrusting sword could fit between the steel plates or through the mail rings of armor.

In the later Middle Ages, some knights carried swords that were so long and heavy they couldn't hold them in one hand. These were called *hand-and-a-half swords*. Hand-and-a-half swords could be nearly as tall as the knights who carried them!

A knight's *lance* was nearly as important as his sword. A lance was a very long pole with a sharp steel point on the end.

A knight on horseback held his lance in one hand and galloped toward his enemy. When he got close enough, he tried to stab his enemy or knock him off his horse with the lance.

Yikes!
Sometimes a whole line of knights charged an enemy with their lances.

Knights had plenty of other weapons, too. A *flail* was an iron ball and chain attached to a handle. The ball was covered with sharp spikes. A *mace* was a big club with a heavy steel head. A blow from a flail or a mace could crush a knight's helmet—and the knight's head inside!

Mace

Flail

Knights also fought with *battle-axes* and *war hammers*. Battle-axes had short handles and broad, sharp blades. A war hammer was like a big hammer, a club, and a knife all in one.

Battle-ax

War hammer

Shields

Along with their weapons, early knights also carried very large shields. The shields helped protect them against the weapons of their enemies.

As armor got better, the shields got smaller. By the late 1400s, most knights did not carry shields into battle at all. They only carried them in special contests.

These contests were often the biggest events of the year.

They were called *tournaments*.

Turn the page to attend a medieval tournament.

THIS WAY

Tournaments

Tournaments began as practice for war. Knights fought each other in big teams. Their battles were called *melees* (MAY-layz). Melees were very confusing. There were

hardly any rules. It was hard to tell which team was winning. So tournaments began to feature two-man contests.

The most popular two-man contest was the *joust* (JOWST). In a joust, two knights tried to knock each other off their horses with lances.

9

Battles and Sieges

At tournaments, knights fought for glory and prizes. When they went to war, they fought for their lives.

Knights went to war for many reasons.

Sometimes they fought to help their king get more land for his kingdom.

Sometimes they fought to win back land that had been taken from their lord.

Sometimes they traveled thousands of miles to fight wars for their church.

Many knights fought their hardest battles close to home. They had to defend their lord's castle against enemy attack.

Sieges

Sometimes an enemy would try to take over a castle by surprise. A castle in England was once invaded by soldiers hiding in a wagon full of hay!

A more common way to try to take over a castle was by *siege* (SEEJ).

During a siege, the enemy army surrounded the castle. They kept people in the castle from coming out. They kept food and supplies from going in.

The attacking army tried very hard to get inside the castle. They often built special weapons to help them. These weapons were called *siege engines*.

Some siege engines were huge. The biggest was called a *belfry* (BEL-free). A belfry was a rolling tower. It was as tall as the castle walls. It could hold hundreds of soldiers.

During a siege, the enemy army would roll the belfry up to the castle walls. Then they would open the top. The soldiers inside would climb out and try to go over the battlements.

A belfry was also called a "cat" or a "bear."

95

Another siege engine was the *battering ram*. The battering ram was a big, heavy log. The enemy pounded the log against the castle gates or walls, trying to smash them down.

Catapults (KAT-uh-pults) were like giant slingshots. They could throw big boulders at the castle walls. They could also throw boulders *over* the walls at the people inside.

Boulders weren't the only things catapults tossed over the castle walls. Sometimes an attacking army threw dead animals inside the castle. They hoped the animals would spread disease. Sometimes they even threw dead people!

Yuck! Sometimes an enemy army even threw human heads over the walls!

Defending the Castle

Of course the people inside the castle didn't just sit there while a siege was going on. They worked very hard attacking the attackers.

Guards shot arrows from the battlements and towers. If the attackers got close enough, the guards dropped rocks and logs down on their heads. Sometimes they poured boiling water or hot oil down on them.

There were often secret passages inside the castle. Some of the passage floors had holes in them. The holes were called *murder holes*. During an attack, guards hid in the passages. They shot arrows or dropped rocks down through the murder holes if an enemy walked below.

The End of a Siege

Sieges often went on for many months. Even if the enemy army never got inside the castle, they could still win the siege.

To surrender means "to admit defeat and give up to an enemy."

If a siege went on long enough, the people inside the castle would starve to death.

Most sieges ended before that happened.

Sometimes the people inside the castle surrendered. The attacking army then took over the castle and all the land around it.

When an enemy took over a castle, they usually held the lord's family and any other nobles inside for *ransom*. That means they would keep them prisoner until someone paid for their release.

Sometimes, of course, the people in the castle defeated the enemy. Most castles had secret doors that led outside. Soldiers could sneak out the secret doors and take the enemy by surprise.

The secret doors were called <u>sally ports</u>.

Sometimes the king or another lord sent help. His army of knights might rescue the people inside the castle. If the enemy was defeated, *they* could be killed, held for ransom—or thrown in the dungeon!

The Dungeon

The dungeon was a prison in the dark, damp basement of the castle.

Prisoners in the dungeon might be chained to the walls all day and all night. Sometimes they were left to starve to death in their chains!

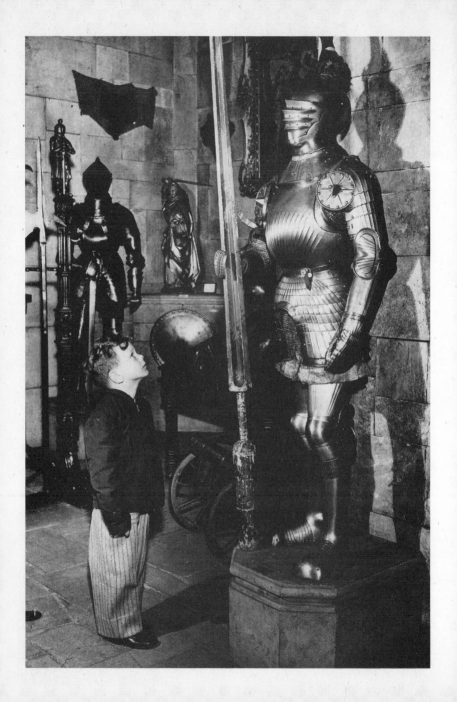

10

The End of the Age of Castles

The Age of Castles lasted nearly 500 years. Eventually, though, people stopped wanting to live in castles.

Castles were dark. They were drafty. They were dirty. They were not built for comfort. They were built for defense against the weapons of a lord's enemies.

As time went by, new weapons were invented. The most powerful of these weapons was the cannon.

Cannons were first used in Europe in the 1300s. By the 1400s, most armies used cannons when they attacked a castle.

Cannons could fire heavy stone or iron balls against castle walls with great force. Even the strongest castles could not stand up against cannon fire for long.

In the late Middle Ages, armies started using cannons on the battlefield, too. At the

A <u>cannon</u> is a large gun, usually mounted on wheels.

same time, soldiers started carrying guns. A knight's armor and his sword were no match for cannonballs and bullets.

The feudal system began to break down. Kings began training full-time armies to defend their kingdoms.

By the end of the Middle Ages, hardly any new castles were being built. And the knight battling in shining armor eventually became a thing of the past.

Knights and Castles Today

Knights and castles live on, though—in stories and legends, and in traditions that are still alive today.

People still become knights. But the people who become knights today don't have to be good fighters. They don't even have to know how to ride a horse. "Knight" is now a title a king or queen can give to anyone who has done a great service for his or her country.

Many castles built centuries ago are still standing. People from all over the world visit these castles every year. The castles often have displays of armor, weapons, clothes, and other things from the Middle Ages.

When you visit one of these castles, you cross a drawbridge into another time.

You can touch the stones carved by masons hundreds of years ago.

You can walk the battlements, where castle guards kept watch for enemy armies.

You can sit in the Great Hall, where pages served lords and ladies their meals on silver plates.

And your imagination can carry you back over 500 years—to the time of knights and castles.

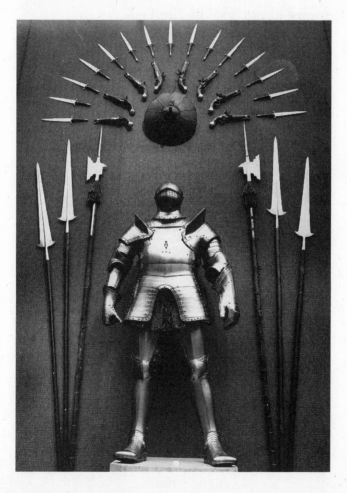

Doing More Research

There are plenty of ways to learn even more about knights and castles.

The fun of research is seeing how many different sources you can explore.

Books

Most libraries and bookstores have lots of books about knights, castles, and life in the Middle Ages.

Here are some things to remember when you're using a book for research:

1. You don't have to read the whole book. Check the table of contents and the index to find the topics you're interested in.

2. Write down the name of the book.
When you take notes, make sure you
write down the name of the book in your
notebook so you can find it again.

3. Never copy exactly from a book.
When you learn something new from a
book, put it in your own words.

4. Make sure the book is <u>nonfiction</u>.
There are many books that tell make–
believe stories about knights and castles.
Make-believe stories are called *fiction*.
They're fun to read, but they're not good
for research.

Research books have real facts and tell
true stories. They are called *nonfiction*. A
librarian or teacher can help you make
sure the books you use for research are
nonfiction.

Here are some good nonfiction books
that tell the facts about knights
and castles:

- *Castle* by David Macauley
- *Castle at War* by Andrew Langley
- *Castles* by Philip Steele
- *Knights and Castles*
  by Avery Hart and Paul Mantell
- *A Medieval Castle*
  by Fiona MacDonald and Mark Bergin
- *Stephen Biesty's Cross-Sections Castle*
  by Richard Platt
- *What Were Castles For?*
  by Phil Roxbee Cox
- *The World of the Medieval Knight*
  by Christopher Gravett

Museums

Many museums have collections of armor, weapons, and other items from the Middle Ages. It's really fun to see things people actually used hundreds of years ago.

When you go to a museum:

1. Be sure to take your notebook!
Write down anything you see that catches your interest. Draw pictures, too!

2. Ask questions.
There are almost always people at a museum who can help you find what you're looking for.

3. Check the museum calendar.
Many museums have special events and activities just for kids!

Here are some museums around the country with good medieval collections:

- Art Institute of Chicago
  Chicago, Illinois

- Cleveland Museum of Art
  Cleveland, Ohio

- Detroit Institute of Art
  Detroit, Michigan

- Higgins Armory Museum
  Worcester, Massachusetts

- Metropolitan Museum of Art
  New York, New York

- Philadelphia Museum of Art
  Philadelphia, Pennsylvania

- San Francisco Art Museum
  San Francisco, California

Videos

Like fairy tales and legends, most movies about knights and castles are fiction. There are some videos, though, that tell the real story of knights and castles.

Check your library or video store for these and other nonfiction videos:

- *Castle*
  from Dorset Video (based on the book by David Macaulay)
- *Knights and Armor*
  from The History Channel
- *Times Medieval*
  from Discovery Communications (The Discovery Channel)

CD-ROMs

CD-ROMs often mix facts with fun activities.

Here are some CD-ROMs that will help you learn more about knights, castles, and the Middle Ages:

- *Castle Explorer*
  from DK Multimedia
- *Destination: Castle*
  from Edmark
- *Nikolai's Knights*
  from H+a
- *Une fete medievale/A Medieval Celebration*
  from Micro-Intel

The Internet

Many Web sites have games and fantasy adventures that feature make-believe knights and castles. When you use the Internet for research, make sure the sites you visit tell the *real* story of life in the Middle Ages.

Ask your teacher or your parents to help you find more Web sites like these:

- www.learner.org/exhibits/middleages
- www.castles-of-britain.com/castle6.htm
- www.castlesontheweb.com
- www.metmuseum.org/collections/department.asp?dep=4

Good luck!

Index

Age of Castles, the,
22, 103
apprentices, 27, 28
armor, 75–81
Arthur, King, 70–73

bailey, 22
barbican, 34, 39
bard, 81
barons, 15–16;
see also nobles
basinet, 79
battering ram, 96
battle-ax, 88
battlements, 32, 38,
97
belfry, 95
blacksmith, 26

Camelot, 70
cannon, 103–105

carpenters, 25
castles, 13–14,
21–53, 103
life in, 41–53
motte and bailey,
22–23
protecting,
31–39, 97–98
stone, 23–27, 31
building of,
23–27
today, 106
wooden, 22–23
catapults, 96–97
cathedrals, 57
chapels, 57
Chivalry, Code of,
68–69, 72
coats of arms, 82–83
craftsmen, 24–29
crenels, 32, 38

Crusaders, 94

dagger, 77
dame, 106
drawbridge, 35, 36,
    39
dubbing ceremony,
    66–68
dungeon, 99–101

feasts, 50–53, 55
festivals, 55
feudal system,
    15–19, 21, 105
fiefs, 15
flail, 88
food, 49–50, 51,
    52–53
freemasons, 25

Galahad, Sir, 72
Great Hall, the,
    48–49, 50, 55, 106

guild, 29
Guinevere, Queen,
    73
guns, 105

hauberk, 76
helmets, 78–79, 81
helms, 78
herald, 83
heraldry, 82–83
high table, 49
holidays, 55
horsemanship, 66

jesters, 51
journeyman, 28
joust, 91

keep, 22, 38
kingdoms, 15
knights, 16, 63–72
    becoming, 64–68
    modern, 105–106

knights *(cont.)*
  names for, 63–64
  role of, 16, 68–69

ladies, *see* nobles
lance, 87
Lancelot, Sir, 72
le Fay, Morgan, 73
lords, *see* nobles

mace, 88
mail, 75–76, 77–78
manors, 15, 16
market days, 58
marriage, 41
masons, 24–25, 26,
  27
master masons, 24
masterpiece, 29
melee, 90–91
merchants, 58, 60
Merlin, 71, 73
merlons, 32, 39

mews, 38–39, 43
Middle Ages, the,
  14–15
minstrels, 58, 60, 69
moat, 34–35, 38
morning star, 88
motte, 22
murder holes, 98

nobles, 18, 19, 41–48
  children of, 44
  clothes of, 46–47
  duties of, 42–43,
   48
  see also barons

pages, 64–65, 69
palisade, 22
pewter, 49
pilgrimage, 57
portcullis, 35, 36, 39,
  78

ransom, 99
religion, 56–57
research, 10–11, 108,
    115
  books, 108–110
  CD-ROMs, 114
  Internet, the, 115
  museums,
    111–112
  videos, 113
rough masons, 25
Round Table,
  Knights of the,
    70–72

sally ports, 99
scaffolding, 25
sentries, 32
serfs, 16–17, 57
servants, 44–45
shields, 89
siege engines, 95–97
sieges, 94–99

squires, 65–67, 68
steel-plate armor,
    77–78, 80–81
swords, 85–86
  hand-and-a-half,
    86
  King Arthur's,
    70–71
  slashing, 85, 86
  thrusting, 85–86

tournaments, 89–91
trade fairs, 58–61
trenchers, 49–50
tunics, 46

universities, 14

visors, 79

war, 14, 93–99
war hammer, 88
weapons, 85–89

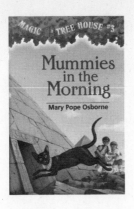

If you liked *Mummies in the Morning*,
you'll love finding out the facts
behind the fiction in

Magic Tree House
Research Guide #3
MUMMIES
AND PYRAMIDS

A nonfiction companion to
Mummies in the Morning
It's Jack and Annie's very own
guide to the secrets of ancient Egypt!

And coming soon...

Magic Tree House
Research Guide #4
PIRATES

A nonfiction companion to
Pirates Past Noon

Other books by Mary Pope Osborne and Will Osborne:

Picture books:

Kate and the Beanstalk by Mary Pope Osborne

Mo and His Friends by Mary Pope Osborne

Moonhorse by Mary Pope Osborne

Rocking Horse Christmas by Mary Pope Osborne

First chapter books:

The *Magic Tree House* series by Mary Pope Osborne

For middle-grade readers:

Adaline Falling Star by Mary Pope Osborne

American Tall Tales by Mary Pope Osborne

The Deadly Power of Medusa by Mary Pope Osborne
    and Will Osborne

Favorite Greek Myths by Mary Pope Osborne

Favorite Medieval Tales by Mary Pope Osborne

Favorite Norse Myths by Mary Pope Osborne

Jason and the Argonauts by Mary Pope Osborne
    and Will Osborne

Joe Magarac by Will Osborne

The Life of Jesus in Masterpieces of Art
    by Mary Pope Osborne

Mermaid Tales from Around the World
    by Mary Pope Osborne
My Brother's Keeper by Mary Pope Osborne
My Secret War by Mary Pope Osborne
One World, Many Religions by Mary Pope Osborne
Spider Kane and the Mystery Under the May-Apple
    (#1) by Mary Pope Osborne
Spider Kane and the Mystery at Jumbo Nightcrawler's
    (#2) by Mary Pope Osborne
Standing in the Light by Mary Pope Osborne
13 Ghosts: Strange but True Stories by Will Osborne

For young-adult readers:
Haunted Waters by Mary Pope Osborne

Where have you traveled
in the Magic Tree House?

❑ #1: DINOSAURS BEFORE DARK

❑ #2: THE KNIGHT AT DAWN

❑ #3: MUMMIES IN THE MORNING

❑ #4: PIRATES PAST NOON

❑ #5: NIGHT OF THE NINJAS

❑ #6: AFTERNOON ON THE AMAZON

❑ #7: SUNSET OF THE SABERTOOTH

❑ #8: MIDNIGHT ON THE MOON

❑ #9: DOLPHINS AT DAYBREAK

❑ #10: GHOST TOWN AT SUNDOWN

❑ #11: LIONS AT LUNCHTIME

❑ #12: POLAR BEARS PAST BEDTIME

❑ #13: VACATION UNDER THE VOLCANO

❑ #14: DAY OF THE DRAGON KING

❑ #15: VIKING SHIPS AT SUNRISE

❑ #16: HOUR OF THE OLYMPICS

❑ #17: TONIGHT ON THE *TITANIC*

❑ #18: BUFFALO BEFORE BREAKFAST

❑ #19: TIGERS AT TWILIGHT

❑ #20: DINGOES AT DINNERTIME

❑ #21: CIVIL WAR ON SUNDAY

❑ #22: REVOLUTIONARY WAR ON WEDNESDAY

A STEPPING STONE BOOK™

Great authors write great books...
for fantastic first reading experiences!

Grades 1–3

Duz Shedd series
by Marjorie Weinman Sharmat
Junie B. Jones series by Barbara Park
Magic Tree House series
by Mary Pope Osborne
Marvin Redpost series by Louis Sachar

Clyde Robert Bulla
The Chalk Box Kid
The Paint Brush Kid
White Bird

Jackie French Koller
Mole and Shrew All Year Through

Jerry Spinelli
Tooter Pepperday
Blue Ribbon Blues: A Tooter Tale

Grades 2–4

A to Z Mysteries series by Ron Roy
Katie Lynn Cookie Company series
by G. E. Stanley

Polly Berrien Berends
The Case of the Elevator Duck

Ann Cameron
Julian, Dream Doctor
Julian, Secret Agent
Julian's Glorious Summer

Adèle Geras
Little Swan

**Stephanie Spinner &
Jonathan Etra**
Aliens for Breakfast
Aliens for Lunch
Aliens for Dinner

Gloria Whelan
Next Spring an Oriole
Silver
Hannah
Night of the Full Moon
Shadow of the Wolf

Grades 3–5

FICTION
Magic Elements Quartet
by Mallory Loehr
#1: Water Wishes
#2: Earth Magic
#3: Wind Spell

Spider Kane Mysteries
by Mary Pope Osborne
#1: Spider Kane and the Mystery Under
the May-Apple
#2: Spider Kane and the Mystery at
Jumbo Nightcrawler's

NONFICTION
Thomas Conklin
The *Titanic* Sinks!

Elizabeth Cody Kimmel
Balto and the Great Race

MARY POPE OSBORNE and WILL OSBORNE have been married for a number of years and live in New York City with their Norfolk terrier, Bailey. Mary is the author of over fifty books for children, and Will has worked for many years in the theater as an actor, director, and playwright. Together they have co-authored two books of Greek mythology.

"We've both done projects in the past that involved medieval times. Mary has retold medieval tales and Will has performed in plays by Shakespeare that take place in the time of knights and castles. Working on this book taught us even more about this amazing period. Our research took us far away, to castles in England and Wales. We also spent time at the armor collection of the Metropolitan Museum of Art in New York City. There we learned that you can slip back into the Middle Ages without going far from home."